LIFE ON A CROP FARM

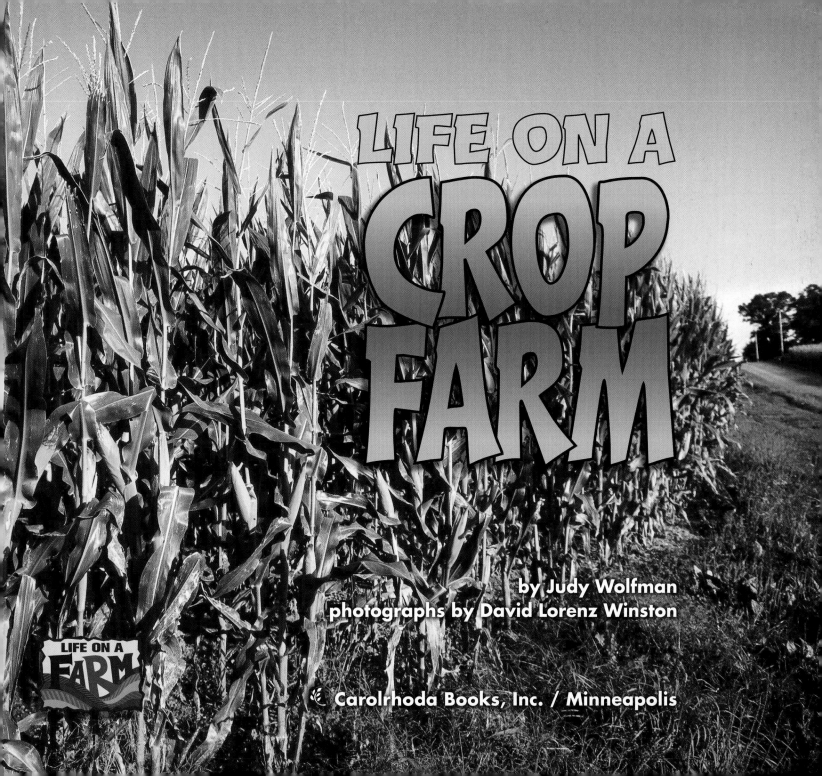

LIFE ON A CROP FARM

by Judy Wolfman
photographs by David Lorenz Winston

Carolrhoda Books, Inc. / Minneapolis

Our thanks and appreciation for the many hours the Lehman family gave us to make *Life on a Crop Farm* possible. Special thanks to Brian for graciously interrupting his work schedule; to Laurie for helping us coordinate schedules; to Melissa, who tells the story; to her sisters, Brittany, Courtney, Brandy, and Tawny; and to her brother, Brian.   —J.W. and D.L.W.

Text copyright © 2002 by Judy Wolfman
Photographs copyright © 2002 by David Lorenz Winston
Illustration on p. 13 by Laura Westlund, © 2002 by Carolrhoda Books, Inc.

Carolrhoda Books, Inc.
A division of Lerner Publishing Group
241 First Avenue North
Minneapolis, MN 55401 U.S.A.

Website address: www.lernerbooks.com

LIBRARY OF CONGRESS CATALOGING-IN-PUBLICATION DATA

Wolfman, Judy.
    Life on a crop farm / by Judy Wolfman ; photographs by David Lorenz
Winston.
        p.   cm — (Life on a farm)
    Includes index.
    ISBN: 1–57505–518–X (lib. bdg. : alk. paper)
    1. Crops—Juvenile literature. 2. Agriculture—Juvenile literature.
3. Family farms—Juvenile literature. 4. Farm life—Juvenile literature.
[1. Farms. 2. Farm life. 3. Agriculture.] I. Winston, David Lorenz, ill.
II. Title.
SB102.W66 2002
630—dc21   00-012470

Manufactured in the United States of America
1 2 3 4 5 6 – JR – 07 06 05 04 03 02

CONTENTS

A Busy CROP Farm

Summer is my favorite time of the year. That's when I can walk outside, pick sweet corn, and eat it right away. It tastes so fresh and delicious! My name is Melissa Lehman, and I live on a crop farm with my parents, sisters, and brother. We grow all sorts of fruits and vegetables, like corn, strawberries, and asparagus. We sell our crops to customers at our roadside stand.

I've lived here since I was two years old, when Mom married my stepdad. (His name is Brian, but I call him Dad.) Our farm used to belong to Dad's grandparents. Dad grew up here and learned how to run the farm by helping my grandfather. Dad and my uncle Bernie do most of the hard work all year long. But when the weather warms up, we kids all have to help, too.

We farm 650 acres. An acre is about the size of a football field, so that's a lot of land.

A farmer's first big job is planting crops in the spring. Crops that have to be planted every year are called **annuals.** Corn, beans, tomatoes, and lots of other crops are annuals. When the growing season ends, these plants die out. That's why they have to be planted again the next spring.

Other crops don't have to be planted every year. They have roots, bushes, or other parts that stay alive over the winter. When spring comes, they start to grow again. Plants that grow this way are called **perennials.** Asparagus, strawberries, raspberries, and blueberries are perennials. Fruit trees are perennials, too.

Corn and green beans are annuals.

Blueberries and strawberries are perennials.

Each year Dad plants the annuals in a different field, or piece of land that has been cleared for farming. This way of farming is called **crop rotation.** Dad says it helps keep the crops healthy. Sometimes insects attack a crop and ruin it. The insects may stay in the soil. If Dad plants the same crop there the next year, the insects will attack it again. But if he plants a different crop, the insects probably won't touch it. That's because each type of insect likes only certain crops.

Crop rotation also helps the soil. Plants take in **minerals** from the soil to help them grow. Each type of plant needs different minerals. Each type also returns different minerals to the soil. If the same type of plant grows in the same field year after year, it will use up the soil's supply of the minerals it needs. And the only new minerals added to the soil will be the ones that the plant provides. So Dad rotates the crops to keep the soil full of all sorts of minerals.

After Dad decides where to put each crop, he's ready to start planting. The ground is usually soft enough to plant in March. Dad goes through the fields with the plow. The plow is made up of blades that turn the soil and break it up.

Next, Dad plants crops that grow well in cool weather, like radishes, broccoli, and cauliflower. These crops have already grown into tiny plants because we started them indoors in our **greenhouse**.

The tractor plays an important part in our work. We can attach many machines to it to do different jobs on the farm. Here Grandpa helps out with the plowing.

The corn planter can plant six rows of corn at a time.

In early April, Dad plants his first field of sweet corn. There are lots of different kinds of corn. We grow sweet corn for people to eat and field corn for animals. Dad keeps some of the field corn to feed to our chickens. He sells the rest to other farmers who don't grow their own corn.

Dad plants the corn with a machine called a corn planter. It has V-shaped blades that make holes in the dirt. Then the planter drops a corn seed, or **kernel**, into each hole. The blades push the dirt back in and close the holes. With this machine, Dad can plant a whole field in just a few hours. I can't imagine what farming was like before people had modern machines! It must have taken ages to plant a whole farm.

The white cloth looks like a giant carpet on the cornfield.

I peel back the cloth to check the corn.
The plants are tiny, but they're on their way.

After the seeds are in the ground, Dad covers the field with a white cloth. The cloth keeps the seeds warm and moist. Soon they **germinate,** or start to grow. Using the cloth gives the corn a head start, so we'll have full-grown plants early in the summer. About every week or two, Dad plants a different field with corn. (By this time, it's warm enough that these fields don't have to be covered.) We'll have corn to harvest all summer long.

Here's a closer look at how a plant makes its food.

The way plants grow is amazing. After a seed is covered with soil, roots sprout from the seed. The roots travel down into the soil. They take in water and minerals. Next, a **stem** grows upward from the seed. Like a straw, the stem will bring water and minerals from the roots to other parts of the plant.

Leaves grow along the plant's stem. The leaves take in water and minerals through the stem. They also take in air and energy from sunlight. (Plants use just one part of air, called carbon dioxide.) Leaves also contain a substance called **chlorophyll**. Chlorophyll makes leaves green. Leaves use chlorophyll, carbon dioxide, and the sun's energy to turn water and minerals into food for the plant. This process is called **photosynthesis.** The food made in the leaves goes up and down the stem, and the plant grows.

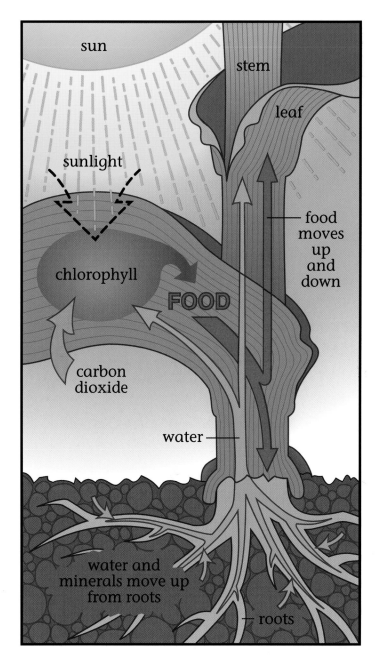

**The asparagus we eat
isn't the whole plant.**
It's just the stem.

While a plant is making food for itself and growing, it also makes food for us. We eat many different plant parts. When we eat radishes or carrots, we're eating a plant's roots. When we eat celery or asparagus, we're eating the stem. Apples and tomatoes are fruits. And lettuce and cabbage are leaves.

As the corn and the other early crops grow, Dad has other plants to think about. Some annuals, like cucumbers, beans, and tomatoes, are planted in April and May. (We get them started in the greenhouse first.) The fruit trees begin to blossom, too. Many of the blossoms will grow into apples, peaches, plums, pears, and apricots.

14

I love the scent of the fruit trees when they blossom. They make the orchard smell so good!

Dad checks the crops as they grow to make sure they're healthy. He uses a machine on his tractor to keep weeds from choking out the young plants. He also sprays the crops with chemicals to keep worms and dangerous bugs away. He sprays the fruit trees to make sure the fruit will be healthy and not ruined by insects or plant diseases.

With so many fields planted with so many crops, it doesn't take long before the food is ready for picking. And that's when work begins for my sisters and me.

15

Plenty of PICKING

It's exciting to see the plants grow and finally be able to pick the food. Picking is my most important chore. It's hard work, but my parents pay me for every basket I fill. So it's like having a job after school and in the summer. I save most of what I earn. When I need spending money, I don't have to ask Mom and Dad.

Three of my sisters, Brittany, Brandy, and Courtney, pick crops too. Our sister Tawny and our brother, Brian, are too young to pick much, but they like to visit the fields. So I have plenty of company. Sometimes we work on our own, but most of the time we pick together. Having someone to talk to makes the time go faster.

Picking is a big chore, but it isn't so bad with my sisters and brother around.

During the picking season, we're in the fields every day unless it rains. On school days, we start picking as soon as we get home from school. We don't even change our clothes. We keep going until everything is picked or until it gets dark. Dad hires a few people to help, but most of the picking is our responsibility. So we put in lots of long days.

Courtney gently breaks off an asparagus stem.

One of the first crops to come up early in the spring is asparagus. Asparagus is easy to pick. We just snap the stems off the plants. (Asparagus stems are called spears.) Each spear should be at least 6 inches tall—we use our fingers to measure. If a spear looks too short, we leave it to grow more. We put the spears in baskets. As we fill a basket, we put it at the end of the row to be picked up later. Asparagus gets picked every other day until mid-June.

We always check the asparagus to make sure it's grown enough before we pick it. These spears are ready to become someone's meal.

It's hard to believe that these tiny white flowers will turn into plump red strawberries!

Strawberries are another early-spring crop. They grow from **runners.** Runners are long, slender growths that look like strings. They creep along the ground and send new roots into the soil. The roots become plants with small white flowers. These flowers become strawberries. As the berries get red, we can smell their sweetness.

Strawberries are one of our most popular fruits. Every year, we hope to get a good crop. But if we have a very rainy spring, the strawberries get too wet and rot. Then they're no good. We can't pick them or sell them. By the time the rainy days are gone, the strawberries are through growing.

I don't like to pick strawberries. Bending over to pick them makes my back hurt. But I love to eat them. The big, ripe, juicy ones are *so* good. Sometimes my sisters and I get bored picking, so we have a strawberry battle. We wear old T-shirts and throw overripe berries at each other. When we come in for dinner, we're a mess!

Strawberries are Courtney's favorite fruit. She's good at picking them, too.

Ouch! If I forget to wear long sleeves and pants to pick raspberries,
I end up with lots of scratches.

Before the weather gets too hot, raspberries are ready for picking. The ripe ones are easy to pull from the stems. But I have to be extra careful not to pull too hard. If I do, the berries get squished. Raspberry bushes are prickly, so I also have to be careful not to get scratched.

Japanese beetles munch on leaves.

Like strawberries, raspberries are sweet and delicious. As I pick them, I sometimes pop one in my mouth—but first I make sure there isn't a Japanese beetle on it. Japanese beetles stick to raspberry leaves and berries and eat them. They're hard to get off. Sometimes they even stick to me, which I don't like at all! If I see a Japanese beetle on a berry, I usually wait for it to fly away before I pick the berry.

While we're picking the early crops, rain and sunlight help the other crops grow. Some years we don't get much rain. Then Dad hooks up the **irrigation** system. It pumps water from our pond to the plants. That way, the crops get the water they need.

What a chore it would be to pick string beans by hand! The picker does a great job for us.

By the end of June, we're in the fields every day. Along with berries, we pick broccoli, cabbage, carrots, peas, squash, and many other vegetables. All the fruits and vegetables have to be picked by hand except the string beans. Dad has a machine called a picker. It has metal fingers that spin around, whack the beans, and knock them off the plant.

Then the fingers bring the beans to the center of the picker.

Next, the picker sucks in the beans like a vacuum cleaner. It takes off the leaves and stems. The beans shoot out the back of the machine into a wagon. Then they're put in boxes. The picker is pretty amazing to watch, and it saves us a lot of work.

The picker shoots the beans back to a wagon. There workers pack them into boxes to be sold.

It's peach time! I'm helping Tawny learn to climb the ladder and pick fruit.

Besides picking vegetables, we also go to the orchard to pick whatever is ripe. We start in June with apricots and peaches. Throughout the summer, we pick pears, plums, cherries, and nectarines.

I like to pick fruit. It's easy to pull from a tree's low branches. But Brittany and I have the most fun climbing our ladders to reach the top branches. I put a basket on top of the ladder and fill it up. One of the adults has to bring it down because it's too heavy for me to carry. Then I move the ladder and climb to another branch.

Brittany is pretty tall, so she's good at picking fruit. Here she's working at an apricot tree.

In late June, the first corn is ready. Of all the foods we grow, I like picking corn the best. Corn grows fast. It can grow 3 to 5 inches a day in the summer! It can reach 8 feet tall. My sisters and I have fun playing hide-and-go-seek in the cornfields while we pick. A stalk of corn has only one or two ears on it, so it doesn't take long to pick. We just pull the ears off the stalk. If an ear doesn't feel full, we leave it so it will keep growing.

There's nothing better than eating fresh corn! It's very sweet. Sometimes we can't wait for Mom to cook it. So we remove the **husk** (the leaves that cover the ear) and eat the raw corn in the field. Of course, we only eat sweet corn—field corn is too tough and doesn't taste good.

Mom says corn
is a good source
of energy. It
has lots of sugar
and vitamins.

I check the corn to see if
it's ready for picking.

Mom's job is to sort the corn into boxes.

29

In July and August, we pick blueberries. They start out as white flowers on the blueberry bushes. When it gets hot, the flowers grow into berries. But they don't all become berries at once. So we go back to each bush several times to pick the new fruit.

Since blueberries have to grow in the sun, we get very hot while we pick them. Sometimes we use umbrellas to shade us. But the worst part is that Japanese beetles love blueberries as much as raspberries. So I really don't like picking them at all.

An umbrella helps block the hot sun while I pick blueberries.

After some of the fields have been picked, Dad turns the soil with the plow. Then he puts in a late crop of fruit and vegetable plants that he started in the greenhouse. These plants give us a longer growing season—and a longer picking season!

Though most of our foods are summer crops, we have apples, pumpkins, and gourds to pick in the fall. The pumpkin patch is fun to walk through. Pumpkins grow on vines that creep along the ground. Each vine is about 10 feet long. The pumpkins begin as blossoms, and usually about six fruits grow on each vine.

You can tell it's almost Halloween when the pumpkin patch turns orange.

Most gourds can't be eaten. People use them for decorations during the fall.

Our customers will turn these pumpkins into jack-o'-lanterns and pies.

Brittany and I try a pumpkin toss for fun.

33

Pumpkins, gourds, and apples are still growing when school starts. So my sisters and I pick after school, like we do in the spring. My teachers say I should do my homework before anything else. But I can only pick crops while it's still light outside. So I pick first and do my homework at night or in the morning before I go to school.

There's more to farmwork than planting and picking the food. We have to sell it, too. At the end of each day, one of the adults picks up the baskets of crops we've picked. The crops are put in a pickup truck and taken to our roadside stand. There we store and sell the food—and that means more work for all of us!

Sometimes an apple grows to a huge size, like this one. But most are more like the ones Courtney's picking here.

**These apples are ready to travel to our stand
to be sold.** I picked many of them myself.

To Market, to MARKET

Our stand is at the end of our lane, not too far from the farm. We live in the country, so some of our customers have to drive pretty far to get here. But since we've had the stand for many years, our food is well known. People keep coming back because they like the food. Sometimes they bring their friends, and we get new customers.

We open the stand in the spring when the first crops come in. In the summer, I try to work there at least six days a week. That sounds like a lot, but it's only for three or four hours at a time. Picking comes first! Sometimes when we run out of something at the stand, I'll run into the fields and pick more so that we're always stocked.

Brian and Tawny play with gourds at the stand.

We sell lots of food at the stand, but almost every week there's some left over. Before it spoils, Grandma takes it to be sold at an auction.

We charge by the pound for foods like tomatoes. I have to weigh them to figure out what the customer owes.

My jobs at the stand are to clean the fruits and vegetables, sort them, and help customers make selections. I show them how to knock on a watermelon to tell if it's ripe or not. A ripe cantaloupe feels rough on the outside and smells sweet where the stem was.

After the customers choose their foods, I figure out what they owe. I give them their change, too. I love math, so I try to do most of the figuring in my head. But sometimes I need to use a calculator. It would be terrible to charge a customer too much money!

By Thanksgiving, all the crops are gone, so we close down the stand. That's an easy job. We just stack up the boxes and baskets and leave. What's left of the plants in the fields are dead, so Dad turns them under with the plow.

He adds **fertilizer**, or plant food, to the soil. Then he puts down **mulch**. Mulch is a mixture of straw, leaves, and earth. It keeps the roots of perennial plants warm over the winter.

It's important to handle the fruits and vegetables carefully. Customers don't want to buy bruised or smashed foods!

I take my time counting money to avoid making mistakes.

Dad also **prunes,** or trims, the fruit trees. He cuts off all the dead branches and thins out the live ones. Pruning allows the sunlight to reach the trees when the growing season begins again. If a tree is too tall, Dad cuts it back. He likes to keep the trees no more than 15 feet tall. If they get taller, sunlight can't reach the lower branches.

We stay busy with more than just crops on our farm. We have about one hundred cows and their calves to take care of. Sometimes I help Dad feed the cows at the end of the day. I also feed the calves twice a day. On weekends, I help clean the barns, too.

These branches have just been pruned.

It's hard to turn around in our barnyard without spotting a calf or a cow.

I love to feed our calves. It's a good change of pace from picking crops!

41

Our farm has other animals, too. We have cats, dogs, peacocks, ducks, and chickens roaming around. They're like pets. We use the eggs that the chickens lay, but we don't sell them.

Our chickens and peacocks make the barnyard a noisy place.

Courtney makes friends with a fuzzy yellow chick.

I like living on the farm. I have a lot of space to play in and plenty to do. I don't mind picking most crops, even though I have to work every day. It's fun to make money and hang around with my sisters and all our animals.

I'm not sure if I want to live on a farm when I grow up, but I hope we'll still have the farm in the family. I'd like to bring my family to visit so they'll know how great life on a crop farm can be.

FunFacts about CROPS

The United States has about 465 million acres of land for growing crops. That's more land than the entire states of Texas, California, Montana, Washington, and Kansas put together!

There are more than 3,500 different ways to use corn products. Corn is used to make **STARCH,** *paint,* film, INK, and **paper!**

Farmers grow corn on every continent in the world except Antarctica.

Prehistoric people began to grow plants from seeds about 11,000 years ago.

The heaviest apple ever grown weighed **3 POUNDS, 11 OUNCES.**

The world's largest pumpkin was grown in Simcoe, Ontario, Canada, in 1998. It weighed 1,092 pounds! *(An average pumpkin weighs between 2 and 4 pounds.)*

Some scientists think that eating blueberries can help slow down or even reverse some of the physical effects of growing old.

In China, people eat candied ASPARAGUS SPEARS as special treats.

Learn More about CROPS

Books

Gibbons, Gail. *The Pumpkin Book*. New York: Holiday House, 1999. This colorful picture book explains how pumpkins are grown and used.

Kudlinski, Kathleen V. *Popcorn Plants*. Minneapolis: Lerner Publications, 1998. Where does popcorn come from? From corn plants, of course! This book shows how a popcorn plant grows from a tiny kernel to an ear of corn.

Patent, Dorothy Hinshaw. *Apple Trees*. Minneapolis: Lerner Publications, 1997. Learn about the growth of the world's favorite fruit through photographs and diagrams.

Richards, Jon. *Farm Machines*. Brookfield, CT: Copper Beech, 1999. Get an inside look at tractors and other farm machines through photos and cutaway drawings.

Websites

Corn World
<http://www.ohiocorn.org/>
The Ohio Corn Growers Association home page offers many fascinating facts about corn and includes activities just for kids.

CyberSpace Farm
<http://www.cyberspaceag.com/>
Explore farming, crops, and farm animals through photographs and games.

John Deere Gallery of Images
<http://www.deere.com/deerecom/_Gallery+of+Images/index1.htm>
View photographs of new and old tractors and other products made by John Deere, one of the world's largest manufacturers of agricultural equipment. Follow the link to the John Deere Kids' Corner, which features stories and kid-friendly information about farm machinery.

Strawberryville
<http://www.calstrawberry.com/>
The California Strawberry Commission's colorful site offers games, activities, and recipes for kids.

GLOSSARY

annuals: plants that grow and die within one year. Annual crops must be planted every year.

chlorophyll: a substance that makes a plant green and helps the plant to make food

crop rotation: planting different crops in a field each year to keep the crops and soil healthy

fertilizer: plant food that helps make soil good for growing crops

germinate: to start to grow

greenhouse: a building where plants are grown

husk: leaves that cover an ear of corn

irrigation: carrying water to dry land through pipes or tunnels

kernel: the seed of a corn plant. Kernels are the part of corn that people eat.

minerals: substances that plants take in from the soil to help them grow

mulch: a mixture of materials such as earth, dead leaves, and straw. Mulch is spread over plants to protect the roots from cold.

perennials: plants that do not die at the end of a growing season. Some perennials have roots that stay alive underground. These plants come up from the ground each year without being replanted. Other perennials, like fruit trees, stay alive above ground all year long.

photosynthesis: a process in which a plant makes its own food

prunes: trims branches off a tree

runners: long, slender plant growths that creep along the ground and send down roots to form new plants

stem: the part of a plant that rises directly from the roots. The stem supports the plant's leaves, flowers, and fruit.

INDEX

About the AUTHOR

Judy Wolfman is a writer and professional storyteller who presents workshops on creativity and storytelling. She also enjoys both acting and writing for the theater. Her published works include children's plays, numerous magazine articles, and Carolrhoda's Life on a Farm series. A retired schoolteacher, she has two sons, a daughter, and four granddaughters. She lives in York, Pennsylvania.

About the PHOTOGRAPHER

David Lorenz Winston is an award-winning photographer whose work has been published by *National Geographic World,* UNICEF, and the National Wildlife Federation. In addition to his work on the Life on a Farm series, Mr. Winston has been photographing pigs, cows, and other animals for many years. He lives in southeastern Pennsylvania. To learn more about Mr. Winston's work, visit his website at <http://www.davidlorenzwinston.com>.